GROWING *Laughter*

CHRISTA PATTON

CREATING LIFETIME CONNECTIONS WITH YOUR CHILDREN

GROWING LAUGHTER
by Christa Patton

© 2014 by Christa Patton

All rights reserved. For use of any part of this publication, whether reproduced, transmitted in any form or by any means, electronic, mechanical, photocopying, recording, or otherwise, or stored in a retrieval system, without the prior consent of the publisher, is an infringement of copyright law and is forbidden.

To purchase copies of *Growing Laughter* in large quantities at wholesale prices, please contact Aloha Publishing at alohapublishing@gmail.com

Cover design by: Dandyline Designs
Interior design by: Fusion Creative Works
Primary Editor: Amy Larson

Print ISBN: 978-1-61206-086-6
Library of Congress Control Number: 2013957196

Published by

Printed in the United States of America

I give great gratitude to my husband, Gregory, and to our two children, Chelsea and Garrett, for this magnificent experience of motherhood.

And to my dad who taught me from the very beginning about unconditional love, patience, and having all the time in the world.

"While we try to teach our children all about life,
our children teach us what life is all about."

—Angela Schwindt

Contents

Introduction	11
Première Partie (Part 1) — LOVE	21
Je T'Aime: I Love You	
Deuxième Partie (Part 2) — CELEBRATIONS	27
Bon Appétit: Enjoy Your Meal	
Les Chansons: Songs	
La Cure Thermale: The Spa Treatment	
La Joie de Vivre: The Joy of Life	
Troisième Partie (Part 3) — GRATITUDE	47
La Reconnaissance: Recognition	
Embrasse La Famille: Cherish Family	
Quatrème Partie (Part 4) — CURIOSITY	57
On Y Va!: Let's Go!	
Les Jeux Amusants: Fun Games	
Tennis N'Importe Qui?!: Tennis, Anyone?!	
Ceci ou Cela?: This One or That One?	
Les Cadeaux Uniques: Unique Gifts	
Cinquième Partie (Part 5) — LISTENING	79
Du Point de Vue d'Un Enfant: From A Child's Perspective	
Les Réalisations: Realizations	
Les Transitions: Transitions	
Remerciements (Acknowledgments & Credits)	157

This is a sacred little quote book that's to be tucked in your night stand—so it's easy to find and always in the same spot. Moms and dads can write in, refer to, get inspired by, and ultimately laugh with their kids through the years within its pages. It's also your creation, an official place to write quotes from your children, from the beginning of their lives through young adulthood. As your child grows, you'll be able to capture the essence of their childhood and your parenting years. With your child's anecdotes, you can record the joy, love, and fun of parent-child relationships. The greatest purpose this book serves is a laughter connection during your child's life (especially during those tough teen years!). When reading and re-reading funny words of their own, your child's quotes will be the source of your future bonding together through shared laughter.

It's been interesting to see how traditions have emerged in our family. While reflecting on these quotes, I've become more aware of their value now that our kids are grown. Realizing, in retrospect, what traditions, or feel-good rituals, we accidentally created gave me the motivation to write this book and share my ideas. It would've been much more fun, as a young parent, to have been consciously aware of how important these little habits and family idiosyncrasies were at the time, and how they would someday blossom into tradition. I didn't realize how much these meant to the kids until they were older. These feel-good rituals are the unique fabric, the very glue that characterize and adhere a family.

The ultimate intention behind this book is to encourage a nurturing relationship with your child. By sharing some simple traditions, we can cultivate strong bonds with our children that get us through whatever challenge life presents, and truly claim the joy we share. I have found no better way to nurture relationships than through laughter!

This is an invitation for you to create what you'd like to see happen in your family, and a way to help develop a long-term vision. Are you a person who believes in writing your own story? It *is* possible to live your life on purpose rather than by chance. Have you thought about playing with your thoughts and dreams, and converting them into your goals and practices?

- What qualities do you want to emphasize and accentuate with your child?

- What things do you want to extract from your own childhood and implement into your child's upbringing?

As the world-renowned author, Stephen Covey, put it:
"Begin with the end in mind!"

Saying French phrases to the kids is one of the traditions that naturally emerged over the years. The French infusion for each chapter title stems from my own love and study of the French language and culture.

- What heritage, language, or even simple movie quotes might you want to infuse into your intimate family life?

- Do you have a thing for Friday night ice cream runs?

- Cranking up the music while doing Saturday chores?

- Do you and your child have a good "talk time" while digging in the garden ~ weeding out confusing thoughts your child might be having?

- When you use nicknames, how does that make your child feel?

- What special meals are prepared for special occasions, holidays, or events?

Look at your family's 'flavor' and 'style.' What makes it tick in a unique way? Become conscious of instilling those things into your own unique style. This becomes the designer glue for the family!

I've included some of my favorite quotes and moments from my children to help inspire you as you use this book.

It all starts with love.

At the core of a family is love, essential for a joyful life. To me, the elements of a family's strength can be summed up with these five words:

Love

Celebration

Gratitude

Curiosity

Listening

Je T'Aime

[jə] [t'em]

I love you

Chelsea said, as I was putting her to bed,
"Mom, I love you around the whole 'versity' and back."
(meaning universe)
(age five)

"You're my best friend in the whole world, mom."
(Garrett, age two and a half)

"Every one of us in this whole world is hooked together in love."
(Garrett, age five)

I said, "Garrett, I love you all the way around my back"
(with my arms stretched out wide).
He replied, "Mom, you love me all around
the whole world ... and that's a lotter!"
(age four)

"Mom, if I had to choose between you and Santa Claus,
I'd choose you for my parent!"
(Garrett, age seven)

Celebration

Bon Appétit

[bɔn] [apeti]

Enjoy Your Meal—Happy Eating!

At a family dinner on Christmas day, Garrett says:

> "Friends are the key to life, and family is the door because they open you up!"
> (age eleven)

Family dinners are a highlight and a daily occurrence. Setting the ambiance with a fire in the fireplace or candles on the table soothes me, so I set the tone. What better way to strengthen the family than over a meal at the end of the day? Gathering together, relaxing, disconnecting from outside demands, and interacting with each other became the binding agent for our family. It's good to get some face time in. Creating this opportunity gives us a chance to engage in good discussion around the table, acknowledging the highs and lows, roses and thorns of our day, and toasting to the day's accomplishments. This is our time to open up to each other.

Les Chansons

[le] [shãsɔ]

Songs

For Mother's Day, at ages five and three, "Chelseabug" and "Gman" gave me a very special gift. They created songs! What made this especially unique is that they matched their made-up song titles to the sounds they created on the piano. Their song titles were:

Key of Wonders
Dinosaurs Sing
Waterfall
Lightening Strikes
Indian Catch
Rainbow of the Dolphins
Flowers of the Heart and Tree of Life

Music is magic. During the day, after school, when I asked them how their day was, they'd say, "Good!" …end of story. But when tucking them into bed at night, I'd start singing a little tune, one that they would finish and fill in the blanks, singing as they told me all about their day. It went like this:

> "There once was a little girl/boy named Chelsea/Garrett, and Chelsea/Garrett had a very busy day…They woke up happy (or grouchy or however they felt) this morning and went off to school to learn and play. They… (pause)…"

They would take it from there and sing to me of the things that were uppermost on their minds, adding in that day's highlights or concerns. Without fail, this connected us, relaxed them, and headed them off into a good night's sleep. Even now, music still connects us, transcending our generations in a way that I don't think any other generation has experienced to this extent. Motown especially moves all ages and stages! What moves you?

La Cure Thermale

[la] [kyr] [termal]

The Spa Treatment

"I love having a tennis player dad and a massage mom cuz I can do a lot of sports, then have a relaxing time!"
(Garrett, age six and a half)

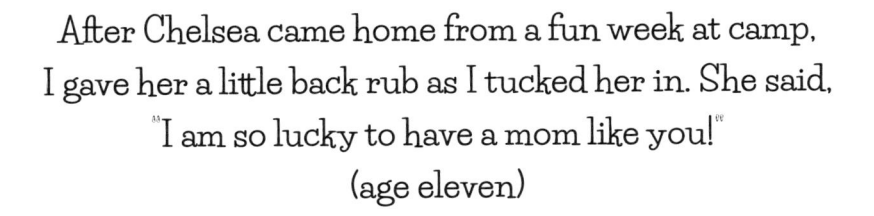

> After Chelsea came home from a fun week at camp,
> I gave her a little back rub as I tucked her in. She said,
> "I am so lucky to have a mom like you!"
> (age eleven)

As a sports massage therapist, I had great creams handy and a massage table. On weekend nights, we would sometimes end the day with "Family Massage."

The idea is that each person got a 10 minute turn on the table to relax. The other three family members would take a foot, arm, head, or back to work on. The kids got to go first. (In retrospect, I would suggest having the parents go first!) This tradition facilitated with teaching reciprocation, family connection, and power of healthy human touch. As the kids got older and more involved with athletics, it also helped with muscle tension and injury prevention.

La Joie de Vivre

[la] [jwa] [də] [vivrə]

The Joy of Life

We watched the celebrations around the world as the clock struck midnight, and Garrett said, "The world is so happy!"
(age eight)

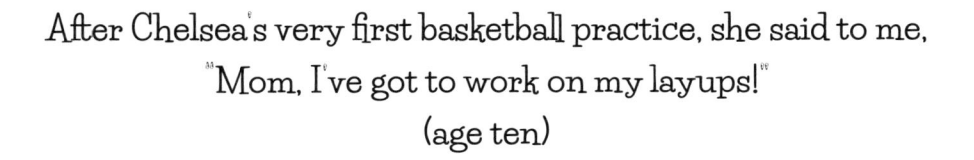

After Chelsea's very first basketball practice, she said to me,
"Mom, I've got to work on my layups!"
(age ten)

We took a bike ride along a winding road in the mountains,
and were almost back to the cabin when Garrett said,
"I feel like a Lamborghini with a half mile left in me!"
(age nine and a half)

I made a 'nest' in Garrett's bed, using a bunch of pillows, of which he said, "Fit for a sparrow!"

Gratitude

La Reconnaissance

[la] [r(ə)kɔnasɑ̃s]

Recognition

Garrett lost his turtle, Zip. That night, he was bummed. He said, "Mom, I don't know if I'm responsible enough to have a pet. It's hard for me to feed him and take care of him and watch him when I take him outside." I said, "I'm here to help you. That's what moms are for."
When saying goodnight I said,
"Thanks for sharing your thoughts."
His response, "That's what Garretts are for!"

Embrasse La Famille

[ãbras] [la] [famij]

Cherish Family

On the way to preschool, Chelseabug (age four) looks out the window and says:

> "Mom, where did all these building and cars come from?
> How did all these things get here?"

I suggested we write to our "GG", her Great Grandmother, since she has seen more development and change over the past century than anyone in our family, having been born in 1907. So that's just what we did! We wrote GG a letter and what a wonderful, interesting note we received in response, one that we've treasured! Her note opened up a whole dialogue about her horse & buggy days, her and Grandy's first car (my Grandad), and their fascination while witnessing the development of airplanes, cities, downtowns, and neighborhoods.

Note writing is another great way to cherish and stay connected with family and friends! Leave notes to family members within the home, and give them to friends and anyone who has done something you appreciate. I have saved many notes that our kids have written on scraps of paper or cards. It's so fun to see the development of their writing style, and now that our children are grown, rereading their funny little love notes these days warms my heart to no end.

Expressing love and gratitude through note writing is something we've instilled in our children. They are really good at it and grasp the importance of it. With all of the tennis tournaments we've gone to and continue to go to, so many people that we've visited have been extremely generous and have gone out of their way for us. Giving gratitude is the cornerstone for continuing to make this possible. Our friends give us great joy, and our lives would be empty without them!

Curiosity

On Y Va!

[ɔ] [ni] [va]

Let's Go!

On the first day of Junior High, "Chelseabug's" adorable, straightforward advice to her younger brother before going off to seventh grade:

> "Little man, if you have a question, ask it.
> And if you have a comment, say it."

Speak up and explore! Be inquisitive! It's a sign of brilliance. "On y va" is used often in our home a phrase to get things moving in a playful way. Whether I just wanted the kids to get in the car, get going, or give encouragement, this phrase serves as a catch-all. The results are excellent, as it's hard to say "on y va" in a caustic tone. Since tone is extremely important to me, and knowing that kids respond much better to gentleness than harshness, softer encouraging words (especially in French!) can have a huge positive impact on a child's self esteem, which is vital to their developing sense of curiosity. Allez! Go!

Les Jeux Amusants

[le] [jø] [amyzã]

Fun Games

"Mom, guess what my favorite animal is?
I'll give you a hint: He has a corn on top of his head!"
I replied, "Of course! A unicorn!"
"Yup, that's it," says "G"!
(age five and a half)

"Mom, are you allergic to elephants?"
"Probably!" I say.
"Ok, we'll just get a bunny then!"
(Garrett, age three)

Coming home from preschool, Garrett says
(in a guessing game type voice),
"Mom, what's the one thing that is great about me?"
I said, "Your smile!"
He chuckled, and said, "Yeah, but what else?"
I said, "Your curly hair."
Gman responded, "No, on the inside!"

I listed: "Your laugh, your jokes..." and finally,
"The way you love your mommy!"
"Yeah!" he responded enthusiastically, "That's it, Mom!"

Games are fun! They don't have to be long or prearranged, just playful! There are guessing games, physical games, games with bouncing balls or balloons, memory games, and countless more that don't require an iPad or internet connection. I learned from our kids that making up games makes the time pass more quickly and makes things a lot more fun while we're all standing in a line, or attending a long event. Games cure fidgety kids!

Tennis N'Importe Qui?!

[tenis] [nẽpɔrt(ə)] [ki]

Tennis, Anyone?

Gman had a late night match in a tournament. Afterward, he said, "My brains and feet got tired, but my arms felt good!"

I was playing tennis with the kids and Garrett says,
"Mom, I'm running ya!" And he was, too!
(age six)

Describing tennis with Dad:
"It was right here in the sweet spot. I had good motion—
my Power Ranger. I hit it cross court and aced Daddy!!"
(Garrett, age six)

"When I'm young I'm going to be a designer and sell my designs.
Then a tennis star. Then after I do all that studying,
I'm going to be an astronaut and fly to the moon.
I've got a full life ahead of me!"
(Chelsea, age nine)

Ceci ou Cela?

[sə si] [u] [sə la]

This One or That One?

The power of choice. What a joy it is when I see my kids make decisions with ease! I truly feel that when little people are encouraged to make small decisions, they will become more comfortable, empowered, and have the self-esteem to make more important decisions as they grow.

> "I used to not like milk and pumpkin pie, but now I do!
> My taste buds are growing!"
> (Chelsea, age eight)

Les Cadeaux Uniques

[le] [kado] [ynik]
Unique Gifts

Creating a memory box for Opa (my dad) was a priceless gift from the heart. It's the sort of gift that everyone in the family can get in on! Each family member puts a unique contribution, story, thought, or memory into the box. For the person who most cherishes family and friends, what a wonderful thing to open! Share the love!

Time on earth is precious.

Listening

Du Point de Vue d' Un Enfant

[dy] [pwẽ] [də] [vy] [d'oẽ] [nãfã]
From a Child's Perspective

"When I grow up to be 100, am I still going to have tangles in my hair?"
(Chelsea, age four and three quarters)

We watched a documentary on Egypt while talking about the Temple of Zeus (origination of Olympics). The narrator said, "...and today the earth has been removed to uncover these ancient ruins."

Gman pipes up, "It's their lucky day!!"
(Garrett, age six)

Mom says, "Please stop rocking on the chair (going side to side)."
G says, "Why?!?" It's fun! You should try it sometime,
Mom. It's good to be a kid sometimes!"
(Garrett, age six and a half)

"I want a Sloppy Joe, Mom." I said, "What's a Sloppy Joe?"
He replies, "It's a hamburger with slop stuff in it!"
(Garrett, age five)

Around Thanksgiving Garrett says, "Mom, you must be part pilgrim because you do a lot of work!"
(age six)

"The one thing I like about corn is that you can eat it like those things that they used to use before computers!" (Typewriters!) (Chelsea, age eight)

"Daddy's a great speaker," Mom says to the kids.
Gman asks, "Does he speak like Dr. Luther King, Jr?"
(age eight)

For Garrett's eleventh birthday, Opa sent a card with eleven dollars in it. When Gman opened it he said, "Wow! This is great! I can't wait till I'm fifty!"

"I just lost my last baby tooth! I'm a real adult now!!"
(Chelsea, age twelve)

When in Hawaii at our Amma ("Godmother") Sybil's "Papalani House," the kids asked, "Do fruit flies ever get tired of flying?"
(Chelsea and Garrett, ages seven and a half and six)

Tucking Garrett in, I said, "Goodnight, Little Pumpkin!"

Without missing a beat, Garrett said, "Goodnight, Big Squash!"
(age six)

"Some boys like to comb their hair and some boys don't.
I'm a don'ter."
(Garrett, age nine)

On the way to school, Chelsea said, "I like my school.
It's a safe and sound school."
(age seven)

Les Réalisations

[le] [realizasjɔ̃]

Realizations—the 'Ahas'!

Counting the twelve days until school was out while sitting at the dining room table, Garrett said, "Mom, every year I feel like I step into a whole new universe...It feels like, WOW!"
(Contemplating third grade ~ age eight)

"When I grow up, will I still be able to be anything I want?" asked Garrett.

"Yes, absolutely," I say.

"Oh good!" he replied,
"I wouldn't want to miss out on any opportunity!"
(Gman, almost nine)

One day we learned that Chinese calligraphy brushes are made out of bamboo wood and animal hair. We talked about the Bamboo Forest in Hana, Hawaii, that we had hiked to. We learned that while in Hawaii, Garrett thought that "Bamboo" was an animal.

Realizations are like bright flashes of joy! To help capture these moments in writing, jot down the priceless times that children experience these bright flashes. Doing mini interviews with the kids is fun, too. Having these instances recorded helps to give children a continuity from their childhood in a way that's unique to each child. They'll see for themselves how they are growing, developing, and coming into their own understanding. This serves as a wonderful self-esteem booster.

> "I have eight Beanie Babies,
> I'm eight years old and I lost eight teeth!"
> (Chelsea)

Les Transitions

[le] [trɑ̃zisjɔ̃]

Transitions

"Mom, usually people grow up in opposite directions...tall and skinny, short and fat...but you're just in the perfect middle."
(Garrett, age eleven)

When learning how to drive my manual car,
Garrett finally mastered a smooth transition while coordinating
shifting and using the clutch and said, "Did you see that?
There was no more of anything!"
(ie: no more car jerking!)
(Garrett, age fifteen)

During Chelsea's first Thanksgiving home from college, she joyfully and gleefully said after two months of dorm life, "I love having a bathroom inside the house!"

Handling transitions means embracing change. If something is changing for the worse, ask yourself, "Where is the silver lining? What can be gained from this unpleasant experience? What's my takeaway lesson to grow and learn?" Be determined to get something positive out of every life experience!

> "Every situation properly perceived becomes
> an opportunity to heal."
> —A Course in Miracles

Share your children's quotes and family highlights on www.GrowingLaughterBook.com

Share your children's quotes and family highlights on www.GrowingLaughterBook.com

Share your children's quotes and family highlights on www.GrowingLaughterBook.com

Share your children's quotes and family highlights on www.GrowingLaughterBook.com

Share your children's quotes and family highlights on www.GrowingLaughterBook.com

Share your children's quotes and family highlights on www.GrowingLaughterBook.com

Share your children's quotes and family highlights on www.GrowingLaughterBook.com

Share your children's quotes and family highlights on www.GrowingLaughterBook.com

Share your children's quotes and family highlights on www.GrowingLaughterBook.com

Share your children's quotes and family highlights on www.GrowingLaughterBook.com

Share your children's quotes and family highlights on www.GrowingLaughterBook.com

Share your children's quotes and family highlights on www.GrowingLaughterBook.com

Share your children's quotes and family highlights on www.GrowingLaughterBook.com

Share your children's quotes and family highlights on www.GrowingLaughterBook.com

Share your children's quotes and family highlights on www.GrowingLaughterBook.com

Share your children's quotes and family highlights on www.GrowingLaughterBook.com

Share your children's quotes and family highlights on www.GrowingLaughterBook.com

Credits

Maryanna Young and the Aloha Team
Sonja Biele
Cory Pironti
Greg Sims
Michele de Reus
Ann Cordum
Amy Larson
Catherine Owens
Elizabeth Mitchell
Chelsey Utsler

About Christa Patton

Christa Patton nurtures her family and friends by giving them unconditional love. She is a big proponent of curiosity and encourages her loved ones to explore life.

In her professional life, she is an associate broker of residential real estate. Her passion in real estate is to help individuals and families move through huge transitions and find a home they can put their heart into. She continues to practice sports massage therapy and, for several years, taught French at Boise State University.

Christa, her husband, Greg, and their two children, Chelsea and Garrett, have a very unique family relationship. They enjoy each other while sharing good meals, traveling, playing tennis, and most of all, laughing and supporting each other through the ebbs and flows of life.

Christa has a Bachelor of Arts degree from the University of California at Santa Barbara, a teaching credential from the University of California at Irvine, and a 'Degre Superieur' from the Sorbonne, University of Paris, France.

She volunteers with Boise State Tennis, Idaho Wheelchair Tennis, and Fort Boise Adventure Waterski Group. Yoga and running with her dogs in the Boise foothills are just a few of the things that keep her fired up. What keeps her constantly inspired are her close friends, family, and anything that's French—magnifique!